Adventures in Writing

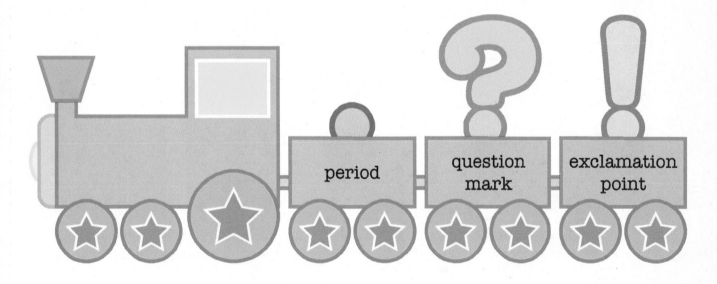

period

question mark

exclamation point

DOVER PUBLICATIONS, INC.
MINEOLA, NEW YORK

Bibliographical Note

Adventures in Writing, first published by Dover Publications, Inc., Mineola, New York, in 2015, contains pages from the following online workbooks published by Education.com: *Introducing the Sentence: First Grade Writing Skills, Sentences: Start to Finish, Good Knight*, and *Time to Write: Dinosaurs and Pirates*, as well as a selection of online worksheets from: education.com.

International Standard Book Number

ISBN-13: 978-0-486-80261-9
ISBN-10: 0-486-80261-2

Manufactured in the United States by Courier Corporation
80261201   2015
www.doverpublications.com

CONTENTS

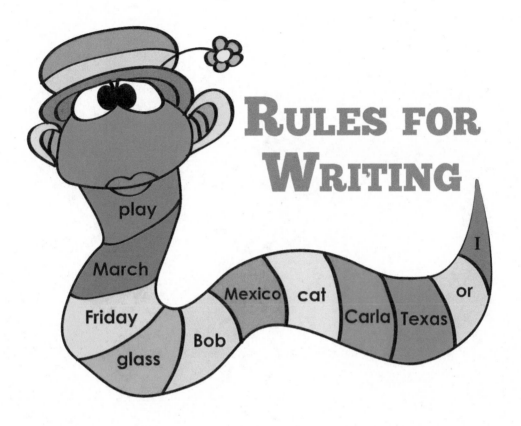

RULES FOR WRITING

Capitalization Rules

Have you ever wondered when to use a capital letter?
Use the following cards to remind you which words to capitalize in a sentence.

Cut out cards

The Beginning of a Sentence

Once upon a time there was a frog.

The Word "I"

Can I have the ball please?

Proper Nouns

My cat Fluffy likes to take long naps.

Holidays, Months, and Days of the Week

My birthday is next Friday!

Proper Nouns

Sally the Silly Snake

Proper nouns are names of important people, places, and things.
They can also be holidays, months, or days of the week.
Proper nouns always begin with a capital letter.
Help Sally the silly snake learn proper nouns.

Color the proper nouns purple. 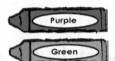 Purple

Color all the other words green. Green

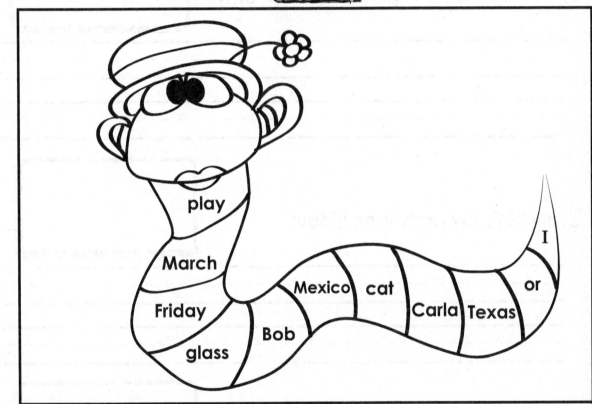

play

March

Friday

glass

Bob

Mexico cat

Carla Texas

or

I

Your Turn!

Now it is your turn. Write 4 more proper nouns.
Make sure they start with a capital!

1. _____

2. _____

3. _____

4. _____

Fix the Glitch

Tips
Use the rules of capitalization to help

Fix It!   Put an X on the letters that should be capitalized.
Write It! Write the sentence correctly.
Draw It!   Draw a picture that matches the sentence.

1. my dog max can play fetch with amy.

2. my birthday party is on friday!

3. when can i go play outside?

Glue It, Write It, Draw It!

Use the words at the bottom of the page to create a sentence. Then glue it, write it and draw it.

Circle all the capitals red.

Circle the ending marks blue.

My   can   Spot

swim   dog   .

7

Glue It, Write It, Draw It!

Use the words at the bottom of the page to create a sentence.
Then glue it, write it and draw it.

Circle all the capitals red.    red

Circle the ending marks blue.   blue

Can

?

I

Tom

play

with

9

Ending Marks
Rules

Tips:

Ending marks always belong at the end of a sentence.
There are 3 types of sentences.

- **Declarative Sentences** tell you who is doing what.
- **Interrogative Sentences** ask a question.
- **Exclamatory Sentences** express surprise, anger, or pain.

Use the following cards to remind you which ending mark to use in a sentence.

Cut out cards

Declarative Sentences

Use a **period**.
Tell us who is doing what.

●

The cat is sleeping.

Interrogative Sentences

Use a **question mark**.
Ask a question.

?

Where is the cat?

Exclamatory Sentences

Use an **exclamation mark**.
Express surprise, anger, or pain.

!

There is my cat!

Sentence Spaghetti

What is a sentence?

A sentence shares a complete thought using words and punctuation marks. A good sentence needs all the right ingredients.

Ingredients

• Start with a capital.

• Write a complete thought.

• Finish with an ending punctuation mark.

Capital

Thought

Ending Punctuation Mark

I like to eat spaghetti .

Ending Marks!

Do you know what an ending mark looks like?

Color all the **exclamation marks green.**

Color all the **question marks blue.**

Color all the **periods red.**

Mark the End

Use the ending marks at the bottom of the page to complete the sentences.
Make sure you use the correct one!

1. Where is my hat

2. The boy is sitting on the bed

3. Let's have a party

 Write one declarative sentence, one interrogative sentence, and one exclamatory sentence.

 _____

? _____

! _____

✂ -

[•]   [?]   [!]

Mark the End

Use the ending marks at the bottom of the page to complete the sentences.
Make sure you use the correct one!

1. Watch out for that tree

2. What day is it

3. I can play the guitar

Write one declarative sentence, one interrogative sentence, and one exclamatory sentence.

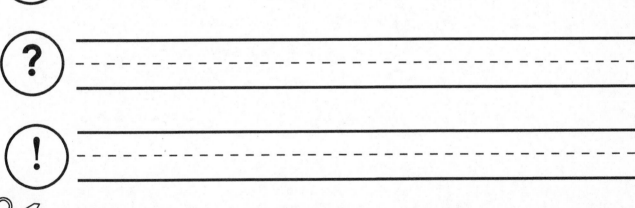

Write Like a Detective

Detectives look for clues to solve a problem.
Can you find the mistakes in the paragraph below?

Draw a  red magnifying glass around all the mistakes, then write the paragraph correctly.

Write the number of mistakes you found inside the big magnifying glass.

	my friend tony likes to play basketball ? we like
	to go to the park and practice on sundays . our
	moms like to cheer for us, "Go, boys, go?"

Magnifying Glass

Write Like a Detective

Detectives look for clues to solve a problem.
Can you find the mistakes in the paragraph below?

Draw a **red** <u>magnifying glass</u> around all the mistakes, then write the

paragraph correctly.

Write the number of mistakes you found inside the big magnifying glass.

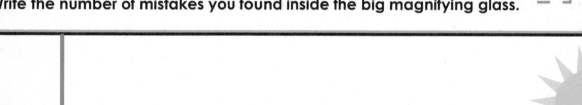

i went to texas with my dad this summer. we saw lots

of things? first i saw the beach! my dog spot liked

playing in the sand. i want to go again next june

Practice Makes Perfect

Great writers spend a lot of time writing and fixing their mistakes.
Write about a time you went on vacation.
Make sure to use all the rules of capitalization and ending marks.
Draw a picture when you are done.

21

Yummy Word Soup

Circle words from the list below and use them to create complete sentences.

Like this: *My dog can play ball.*

Make sure to only use words from the list. How many different sentences can you make?

my	down	one	ball	so	little
and	a	in	you	her	cat
is	up	away	look	for	funny
play	dog	see	big	with	this
we	where	said	he	see	from
me	can	to	she	I	jump

Picture This

Look at each picture and write a matching sentence.
Make sure to use capitalization and ending mark rules.

Picture This

Look at each picture and write a matching sentence.
Make sure to use capitalization and ending mark rules.

Complete Sentences
Rules

Tips:

Good writers always use complete sentences.

Use the cards below to help you remember the difference between a complete and an incomplete sentence.

Cut out cards

Complete Sentences

- Share a complete thought.
- Use many details.
- Tell us *who* did *what* and *where*.
- Use capitalization and ending mark rules.

The boy is reading quietly on the floor.

Incomplete Sentences

- Do **NOT** share a complete thought.
- Do **NOT** use details.
- Do **NOT** use capitalization and ending mark rules.

Boy   on   floor

Color If Complete

Read the sentences below and decide if they are complete or incomplete.

Color the complete sentences yellow   ◁ yellow
Put an **X** on the incomplete sentences.

The dog is playing ball outside.	I found 2 pens!
My mom is cooking dinner.	Where is it?
the house big!	I can make a pizza.
Can Ben come out and play?	Linda likes to dance.
We can make a pie tomorrow.	John can help us clean too.
Pick up.	The cat is sleeping on the couch.
His house outside	It is not fair.
Bring it to me.	He smart boy.

Fix the Glitch

All these sentences are incomplete.
Can you help us fix them? Make sure to use lots of details.
Draw a picture when you are done.

1. Cooking a pizza.

2. Colored a picture.

4. Playing outside.

Practice Makes Perfect

Great writers spend a lot of time writing and fixing their mistakes.
Write about a time you went on a field trip.
Make sure to use complete sentences.
Draw a picture when you are done.

Great job!

_____

is an Education.com writing superstar

Writing Skills

Punctuation Fill-In

Fill in the blanks. Use a period, exclamation point, or question mark. In some cases, more than one type of mark can be correct.

1.) The car is red____

2.) Where is the dog____

3.) I love ice cream____

4.) What time is it____

5.) You're great____

6.) Cats like milk____

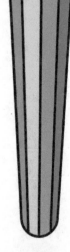

Punctuation Match-Up

Match each punctuation mark to its name.

question mark

period

exclamation point

comma

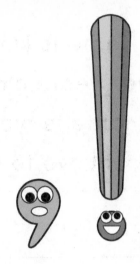

Write your own sentence, using at least one punctuation mark.

Correct the Capitals

Re-write the passage below.
Correctly capitalize the words.

my Name is kimiko. i'm from japan. i'm
Seven years old and i have one brother.
his name is ryo. we live in a City called
nara. i Love to sing and play Tennis.

Correct the Capitals

Re-write the passage below. Correctly capitalize the words.

Hi, Mom!

once upon a Time, there was a boy named frank. frank wanted to Be an astronaut and visit the Moon. he hoped one day he would see earth from Space.

SCIENCE TIME : EARTH

Our planet Earth is made up of four major layers. The thin, outermost layer where we live is called the **CRUST**. Beneath the crust is a rocky shell called the **MANTLE**. The next layer down is the **OUTER CORE**, which is liquid. Below the outer core is the **INNER CORE**. The inner core is solid. Label each layer of the Earth below using what you've learned.

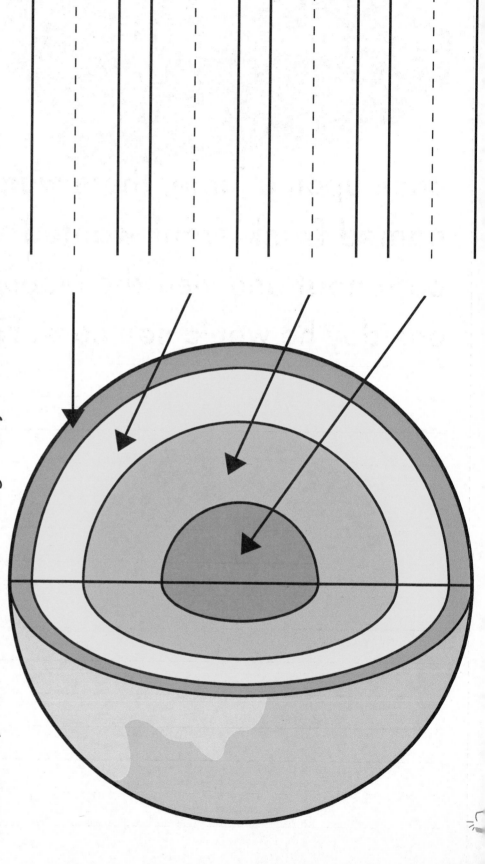

SCIENCE TIME : THE SUN

The Sun is the star at the center of our Solar System which provides us with light. The Sun's outer layer is called the **CONVECTIVE ZONE**. The next layer is the **RADIATIVE ZONE**. The innermost layer of the Sun is called the **CORE**. Label each layer of the Sun below using what you've learned.

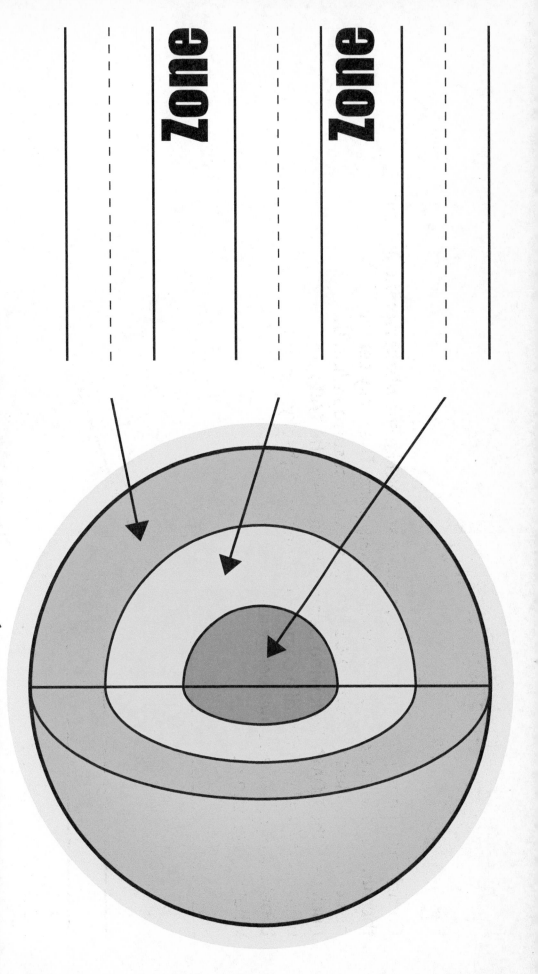

_____ Zone

_____ Zone

_____

SCIENCE TIME : COMET

Comets are members of the solar system that look like snowballs zipping around the sun. Comets are composed of three main parts. The rocky center of a comet is called the **NUCLEUS**. The gas and dust surrounding the nucleus is the **COMA**. Following behind the coma is the **TAIL**, which is the easiest part of a comet to see in the night sky. Label each part of a comet below using what you've learned.

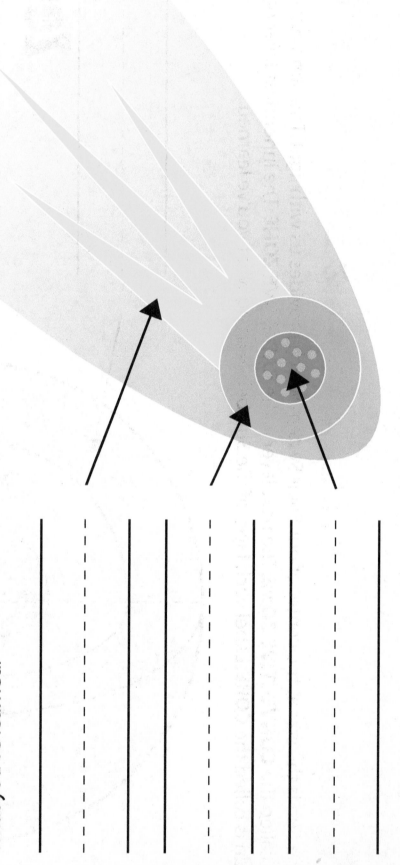

Using Sight Words

Write four sentences using one of the words from the box in each sentence.

any	them	over	let

Using Sight Words

Write four sentences using one of the words from the box in each sentence.

as   think   live   could

Using Sight Words

Write four sentences using one of the words from the box in each sentence.

take	of	some	has

Using Sight Words

Write four sentences using one of the words from the box in each sentence.

going	when	stop	just

Using Sight Words

Write four sentences using one of the words from the box in each sentence.

thank	once	were	his

It's raining, it's pouring...

What do you like to do on a rainy day?

How's the weather today?

Write a sentence describing the weather shown.

How's the weather today?

Write a sentence describing the weather shown.

How's the weather today?

Write a sentence describing the weather shown.

How's the weather today?

Write a sentence describing the weather shown.

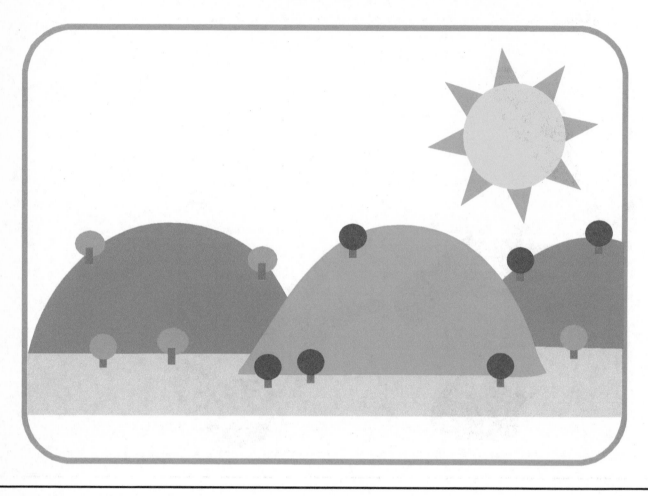

Have you ever seen a giraffe drink water? Where?

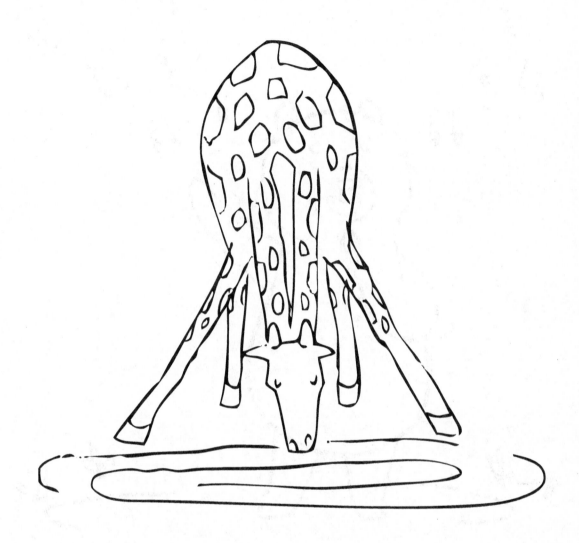

Write a story below:

_____

_____

_____

_____

_____

51

What is this bear doing?

Write a story below:

_____

_____

_____

_____

_____

Great job!

is an Education.com writing superstar

Sentences: Start to Finish

Start with a Capital Letter

The first word in a complete sentence must begin with a capital letter.

Circle the sentences that start with capital letters.

Dinah loves to knit.   The cat caught a mouse.   i like eating cheese.

Today is a nice day.   yesterday was rainy.   I am going on a picnic.

i have the movie tickets.   The park was fun.   the dog is fast.

I like reading books.   Bobby dropped the ball.   my cat likes to watch birds.

Rewrite each sentence so that it begins with a capital letter!

1. the cat played with a ball of yarn.

_____

2. the cat and the dog chased after a bird.

_____

3. i just bought an ice cream cone.

_____

4. i would like another piece of cheese.

_____

Capitalization

Carol and her cat need help with capital letters. Help them make each sentence correct by circling the letters that need to be capitalized.

1. david ate lunch with me.

2. Amy and i are going to the movies.

3. My dog's name is comet.

4. samantha does gymnastics with jack.

5. We are going to hawaii for vacation.

6. Tomorrow i am having a party.

7. where is the bathroom?

8. my birthday is in december.

9. brian and justin are brothers.

10. We're going to new york in june.

Capitalize It!

The first letter of a sentence, names of people and places, and the word "I" are all capitalized. Fix the sentences below so they are capitalized correctly.

sammy wears his new raincoat to school today.

_____.

mary bought some chocolate truffles.

_____.

i took tabby to see the veterinarian yesterday.

_____.

mr. mcdermott is a plumber.

_____.

i went to the lincoln park zoo to see a hedgehog.

_____.

the rockets beat the jaguars in the basketball game last night.

_____.

Complete or Incomplete

Write "c" if the sentence is a complete sentence.
Write "i" if the sentence is an incomplete sentence.

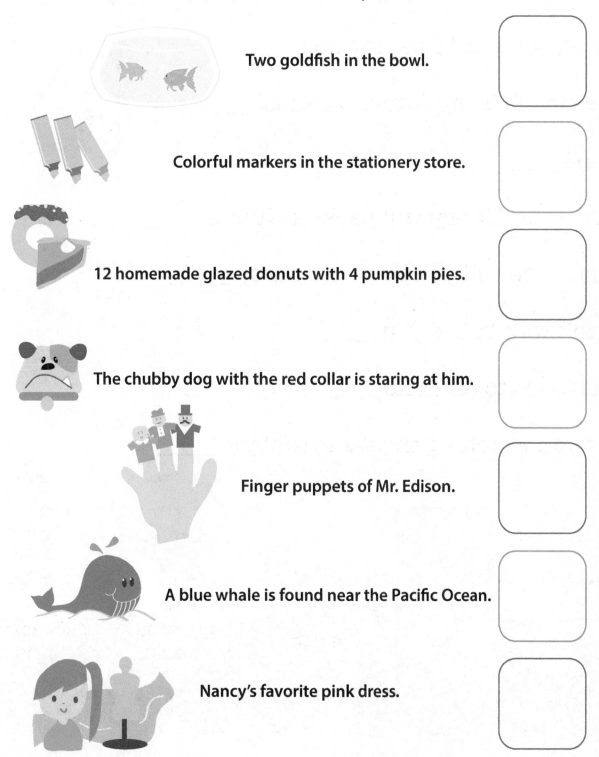

Two goldfish in the bowl.

Colorful markers in the stationery store.

12 homemade glazed donuts with 4 pumpkin pies.

The chubby dog with the red collar is staring at him.

Finger puppets of Mr. Edison.

A blue whale is found near the Pacific Ocean.

Nancy's favorite pink dress.

PUNCTUATION STATION

Fill in the blanks below with a period, question mark or exclamation point. In some cases, more than one can be correct.

1. Would you like to pet my dog _____

2. The giraffe is my favorite animal _____

3. Oh no_____

4. Tomorrow Henry will pack his lunch _____

5. What time will you be at the party _____

6. I can't wait to see you _____

7. Tina loves to eat cake _____

8. Are you watching the game tonight _____

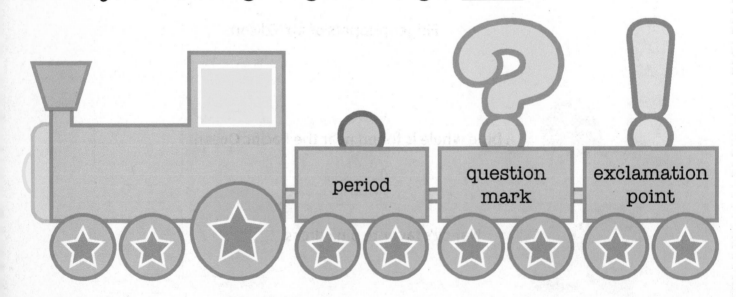

period   question mark   exclamation point

High Frequency Sight Words

Choose a word from the bubbles below. Use a word to complete each sentence.

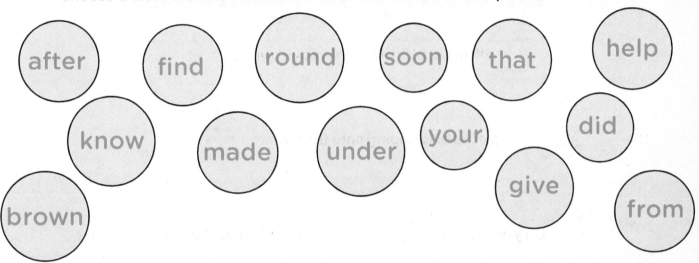

I got a cookie _____ the store.

I _____ a yummy snack.

Is that _____ favorite book?

My shoes are _____ the bed.

The dog has _____ fur.

I like to _____ cook dinner.

Did you _____ my red hat?

Making Sentences

Fill in the blank with the correct word.

The _____ (cat/cats) is leaping onto the fence.

Lucy bought two _____ (necklace/necklaces) for her sister.

There are many beautiful _____ (picture/pictures) in the gallery.

The witch changed the prince into the _____ (frog/frogs).

At the campground, boy scouts are building _____ (tent/tents).

Tammy lost her _____ (wallet/wallets) on the way to school.

A pair of _____ (mitten/mittens) can keep you warm in the winter.

Punctuation: In the Garden

Every statement ends with a period. Every question ends with a question mark. Add a period or question mark to the end of each sentence.

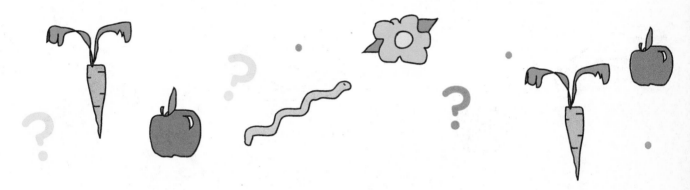

Do you see the worms ____

I like growing carrots ____

An apple fell from a tree ____

Is the sun out ____

The flowers are pink ____

A bird dropped a seed ____

Where is the shovel ____

Today is a nice day ____

Planting a garden is fun ____

Lunchroom Punctuation!

Add in the correct punctuation by writing a question mark,
exclamation mark, or period at the end of each sentence.

What is your favorite sandwich ____

My favorite snack is cheese ____

I can't wait to eat my cookies ____

How many apples are on the table ____

Did you drink your juice box ____

I am excited about snack time ____

I like to drink milk with a straw ____

May I have another helping of pie ____

Today's lunch is tomato soup ____

Sentence Types

Add the correct ending onto each sentence.

Put **.** *if the sentence is a **declarative** sentence, or a sentence that makes a statement.*
Put **!** *if the sentence is an **exclamatory** sentence, or a sentence that expresses a strong feeling.*
Put **?** *if the sentence is an **interrogative** sentence, or a sentence that asks a question.*

The prince is going to rescue a princess who is locked up on the mountain ☐

He has gathered all his weapons to slay the dragon who guards the princess ☐

When he gets there, he sees the dragon and gets scared ☐

"What should I do ☐ " he says ☐

Suddenly, a fairy appears ☐

She says, "Don't worry, I can help you with my magic ☐ "

With the help of the fairy, the prince tames the dragon and rescues the princess ☐

The prince and the princess live happily every after ☐

65

Write A Sentence

There are three main types of sentences:
A *declarative* sentence, or a sentence that make a statement.
An *exclamatory* sentence, or a sentence that expresses a strong feeling.
An *interrogative* sentence, or a sentence that ask a question.

Use each picture on the left to write a declarative, exclamatory, and interrogative sentence. Don't forget to punctuate correctly.

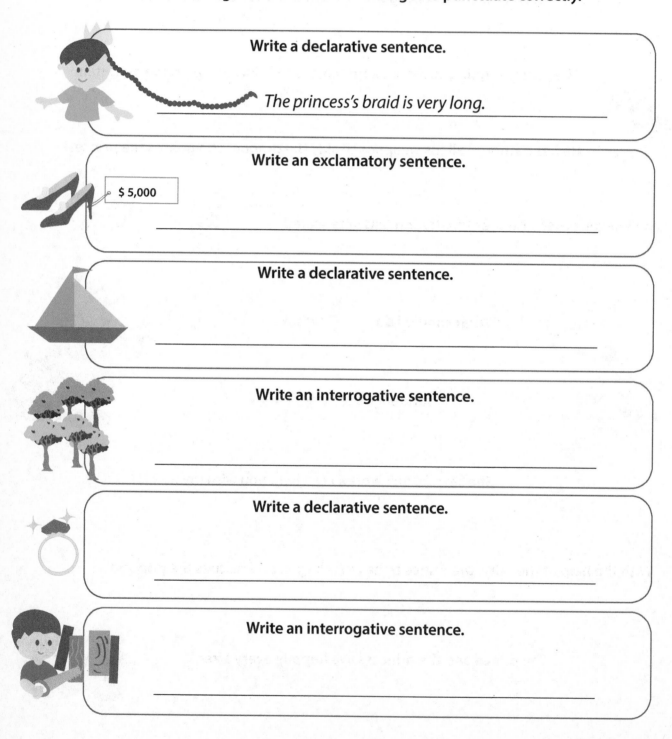

Write a declarative sentence.

The princess's braid is very long.

Write an exclamatory sentence.

$ 5,000

Write a declarative sentence.

Write an interrogative sentence.

Write a declarative sentence.

Write an interrogative sentence.

Building Sentences

Every sentence has two parts. The **naming part** tells who or what the sentence is about. The **action part** tells something about the naming part. A **naming part** and an **action part** make a complete thought.

Each idea below needs a naming part or an action part. Add words to each line to make a complete sentence.

1. The cat _____ .

2. Anna _____ .

3. _____ plays outside in the park.

4. The two girls _____ .

5. The new garden _____ .

6. _____ jumps in the swimming pool.

7. _____watch the ducks.

8. The flowers _____ .

9. _____ run in the grass.

10. _____ pet the new puppies.

 # Creative Writing

Feelings

Complete the sentences below.

1. One thing that makes me feel happy is _____

_____

2. When I'm sad something that makes me feel better is _____

_____

3. Being around my friends and family makes me feel _____

_____

4. I get really scared when _____

_____

5. When I feel hungry I eat _____

_____

6. When I'm bored I like to _____

_____

7. I feel really silly when _____

_____

Creative Writing

Sports

Complete the sentences below.

1. My favorite sport is _____ because

_____

2. I like to play my favorite sport with _____

_____

3. To play my favorite sport I need to use _____

_____

4. The person who taught me to play sports is _____

_____

5. Playing sports makes me feel _____

_____

6. The hardest part of playing sports is _____

_____

7. The most fun part of playing sports is _____

_____

The Bookstore

Some of these are complete sentences and some are not.
Underline the complete sentences.

I like to go to the bookstore.

My mother, my sister, and I.

We looked at the new books.

The books on the shelf.

I love to read mystery books.

My mom likes cookbooks.

The blue book cover.

We bought four great books.

Are good books.

COMPLETE SENTENCES

A complete sentence has a subject and a verb. Add a subject or a verb from the word bank to each sentence to make it into a complete sentence.

Example: The boy in the blue shirt
The boy in the blue shirt is running in the playground.

The dog	stands in line	The fish	Birds are	is the smallest
The family	It is hot	The neighbors	It snows	The glass

1.   swims in the lake

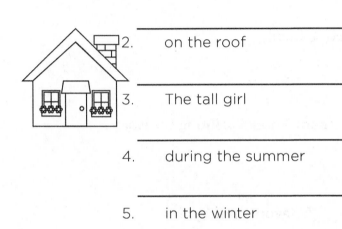

2.   on the roof

_____

3.   The tall girl

_____

4.   during the summer

_____

5.   in the winter

_____

6.   went on vacation

_____

7.   at the airport

_____

8.   drinks the water

_____

9.   The brown puppy

_____

10.   fell and broke

_____

71

Complete It!

The subject is the who or what of a sentence.
Write the missing subject to make the sentence complete.

Tammy and Joey _____ are singing together in front of the class.

_____ is jumping so high!

_____ spent 3 hours painting the wall.

Knitting is one of _____'s favorite hobby.

_____ will join the school band this year.

_____ grows a lot of cabbage on his farm.

_____ floats across the sky.

Questions, Questions...

A sentence that asks something is called a **question**.
A **question** begins with a capital letter and ends with a **question mark**.

Circle the questions.

I went to the store.   Do you like cookies?   School is fun.   Are you tired?

The cat is furry.   Did you see the dog?   How many pies will you make?

The weather is warm.   Will it rain today?   I like to eat apples.   How are you?

These questions are written incorrectly.
Rewrite each question correctly.

1. do you like bananas

_____

2. where is the school bus

_____

3. did you pass the test

_____

Punctuation

Pedro the Parrot needs help putting the correct punctuation at the end of each sentence. Help him complete each sentence by adding a period (.), exclamation point (!), or question mark (?).

1. When is your birthday _____

2. I love ice cream _____

3. My favorite subject is writing _____

4. Sam walks to school _____

5. How far can you run _____

6. The dog is in the dog house _____

7. What is the title of the book _____

8. We had pizza for lunch _____

9. May I have a drink of water _____

10. The cat jumped on the fence _____

Great job!

is an Education.com writing superstar

Good
Knight

Rescue the Prince!
Maze

Help the brave princess find her way through the castle to the prince, but be careful to avoid the dragon!

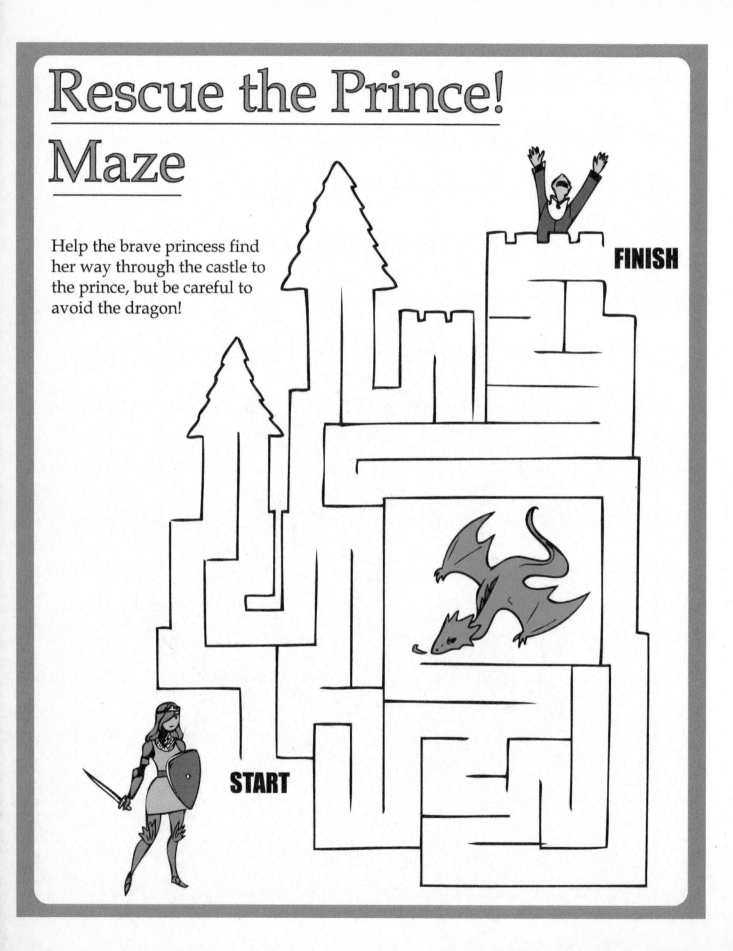

FINISH

START

Dragon Mobile

Directions:

1. Cut out the dragon's body and wings.
2. Use a gluestick to paste the two sides of the dragon's body together.
3. Fold the tabs of the wings down at the dotted line, and glue them to opposite shoulders at the dotted line.
4. Puncture a hole in the dragon's back at the dot, and thread string through to hang!

Color me!

Escape the Castle Labyrinth!

FINISH

START

Castle Pop-Up Directions:

1. Color and cut out the castle.

2. Fold dotted-line A into the castle; make sure to crease the fold well! Then unfold the sheet.

3. Fold dotted-line B into the castle, and then unfold.

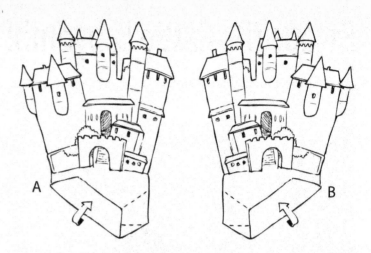

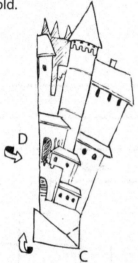

4. Fold dotted-line C into the castle, DO NOT unfold the sheet.

5. Now fold dotted-line D, so that when you look at the paper folded, the castle illustration is face out.

6. Fold a sheet of construction paper in half, hamburger or hot dog style.

7. With a gluestick, glue only the underside of the green section of the castle cutout!

8. With your folded construction paper facing you like a book, fit the castle into the crevice made by the fold, making sure the paper is tucked tightly into the crevice of the construction paper.

9. When the 'book' is open wide, the castle cutout should be creased facing the opposite way of the construction paper. The castle will collapse forward into the book when closed.

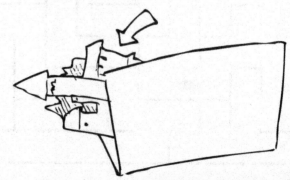

Castle Pop-Up

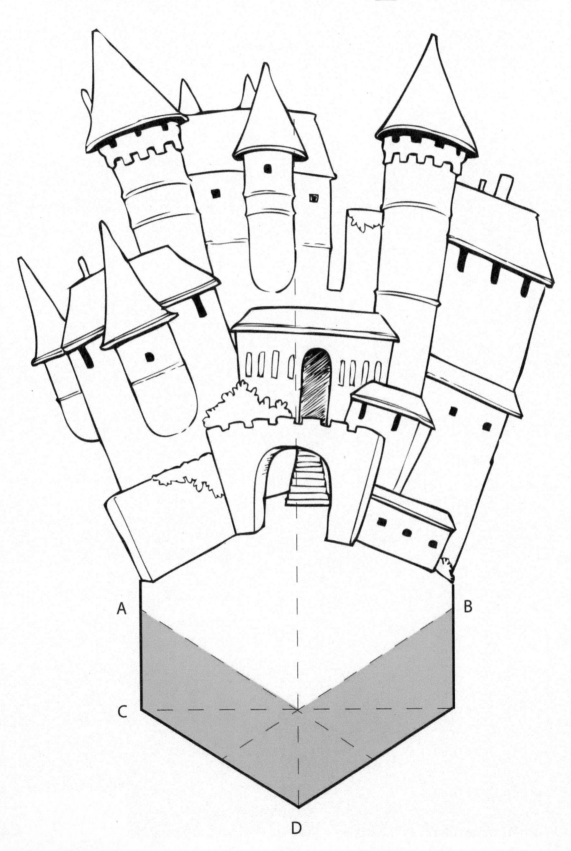

A

B

C

D

Cube Knight

1. Cut out cube shapes and fold along dotted lines.
2. Fold black tabs inwards and glue.
3. Glue surfaces with letters x, y, z to matching spaces.

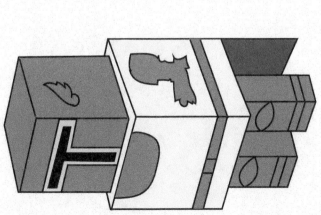

Rapunzel Math!

Directions: Rapunzel must let down her hair so the prince can climb up to her window! Use a ruler to measure how long her hair is. Start from the top of her head, to the bottom tip of her hair. Measure the length in both inches and centimeters.

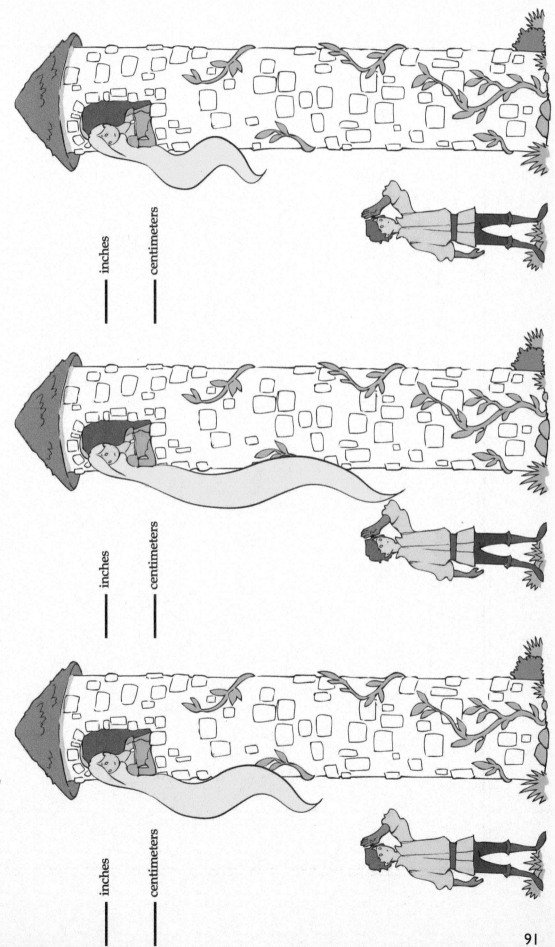

_____ inches

_____ centimeters

_____ inches

_____ centimeters

_____ inches

_____ centimeters

Mixed Up Fairy Tales

Something is off...
This brave knight has found her way to the beautiful, sleeping... prince? Color in the picture and write a story about "Sleeping Handsome".

92

What's Going On?

Use the next page to create a story about the image below. Be sure to create a story with a proper beginning, middle and end.

Creative Writing

Creative Writing

Create a story of the scene below on the next page. Use the empty box to create another character. It can be a dragon or some kind of monster. Be sure to include descriptive words to create your story.

Creative Writing

Know Your "Kn-" Words!

Chainmail Art

Tools do more than just fix things! This art project will give your child the opportunity to build up his knight's strength using metal washers, screws, bolts and aluminum foil, creating the most resistant armor anyone has ever seen. This knight made with actual tools is the strongest you'll ever see.

What You Need:

- 18" x 9" foam board
- Tempera paint
- Nuts, bolts, screws, washers in a variety of small sizes
- Aluminum foil
- Scissors
- White glue
- Paintbrushes
- Pencil

What You Do:

1. Have your child paint the foam board red and allow it to dry. Paint a second coat if necessary.

2. Draw the basic outline of the knight onto the dried, painted foam board. Make sure to include the knight's helmet, face, sword, shield and pointed shoes.

3. Now he can paint in the knight's face by mixing a small amount of white and yellow ochre together to create a flesh color. Paint in his eyes and mouth too.

4. Start assembling the nuts, bolts, screws and washers where you want them to go, filling in the pencil line of the knight. Round washers work well for jointed areas, such as shoulders, elbows, knees and ankles.

5. Once they are arranged exactly how you want them, glue them in place, one piece at a time.

6. Cut the aluminum foil into strips and then into squares. Fit it inside the lines of the knight to complete his heroic outfit. Place a thin layer of glue where you want the aluminum foil to go. Gently press the foil down in place.

7. Go back in with a colored paint to add details to the shield and sword.

Your knight is ready to defend! Hang him somewhere you can use protection or the outside of your door to keep intruders away!

Rapunzel Card Craft

Rapunzel, Rapunzel, let down your hair! This greeting card is perfect for any little princess, or one of the ladies in her royal court. Watercolor paper, paint, felt, braided yarn and a limitless imagination are all your child needs to bring this fair-haired maiden to life. Rapunzel's tall tower creates the base for the card, and her signature blond hair cascades out the window. This is the perfect craft to share with any budding bookworm.

What You Need:

- 2 sheets Watercolor paper (8.5 inches x 11 inches)
- Watercolor paint
- Brushes
- Paper Towel
- Black Marker

- Glue stick
- Yellow yarn, 6 strands each cut at 24" long Brown Felt
- Markers
- Stapler
- Tape

What You Do:

1. Help your child fold both sheets of watercolor vertically, so they are tall and thin. Place one folded card to the side.

2. Fold one half of the folded card in half once again, creating a fold that is 1/4th the size of the paper. Cut the 1/4th segment out with a pair of scissors. Set the rest of the cut sheet of paper aside for another project. The remaining piece will become the top of the tower.

3. Attach the tower extension to the inside top of the folded card using a staple to keep it in place. Tape over the staple to secure the tower at the top of the card.

4. Brush clear water over the entire card.

5. Paint into the water with watercolor paints. Paint the tower with gray paint. Bunch up a paper towel and blot the gray color while it's wet to give it the texture of stone. Make sure to leave a window at the top of the tower for Rapunzel to sit. Paint the land around the tower with flowers, grass and blue skies. Set aside to dry.

What You Do:

6. Gather the yarn and tape one end together. Separate the yarn into three sections.

7. Help little fingers braid the yarn until you reach the end. Tie the end into a knot. Cut the tape off of the other end and tie it in a knot.

8. Cut an oval out of the felt for Rapunzel's face and glue it in the tower.

9. Draw her face onto the felt.

10. Outline the stones on the tower with a black marker.

11. Glue the center of the braid at the top of her head. Glue the braid in place on the card.

12. Write a secret message and give your Rapunzel card to a friend who you love!

Great job!

_____

is an Education.com writing superstar

Time to Write: Dinosaurs and Pirates

Give this pirate and his trusty T-rex names! Where are they going?
How do you think they met and became friends?

Pirate's Name: _____

T-rex's Name: _____

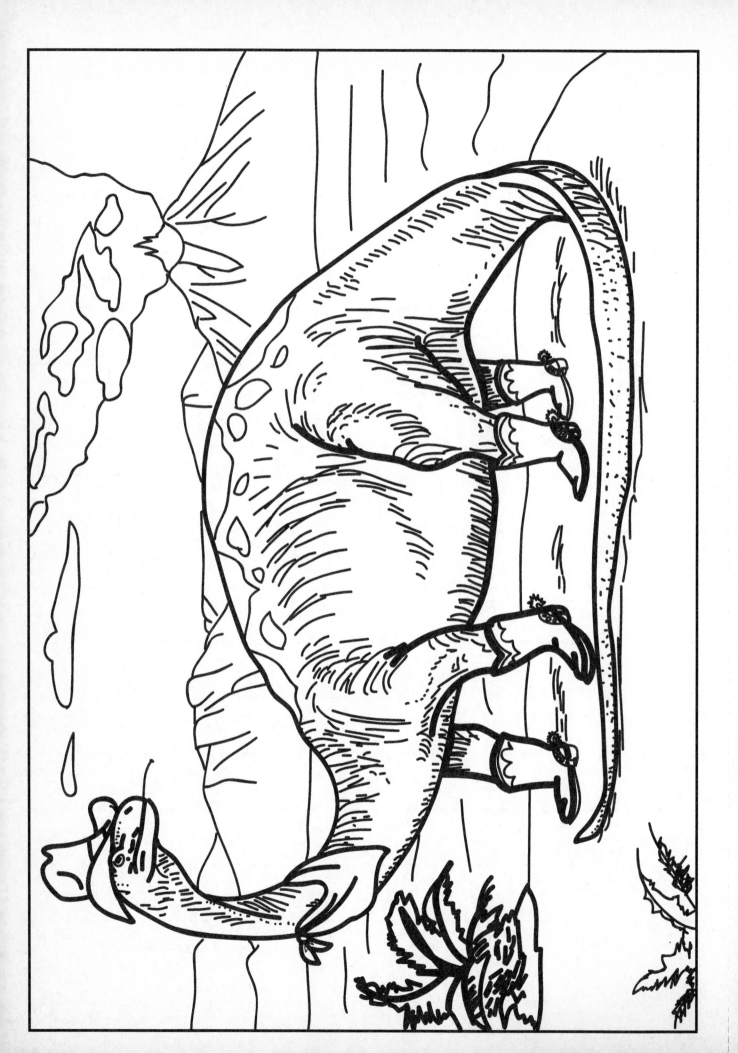

Bronk the Brontosaurus would like to be your friend! If you could be any dinosaur, which prehistoric creature would you be and what would be your name?

Build a Dinosaur-Pirate!

Build and color a PIRATE-SAURUS Rex!
Have an adult help you cut out Captain
Dino Claw and his accessories. Then see
what wild and fun creations you can come
up with! To keep the creativity going, use
the last page to write a fun story for your
new swashbuckling friend.

Cut along the dotted line.

Captain
Dino Claw

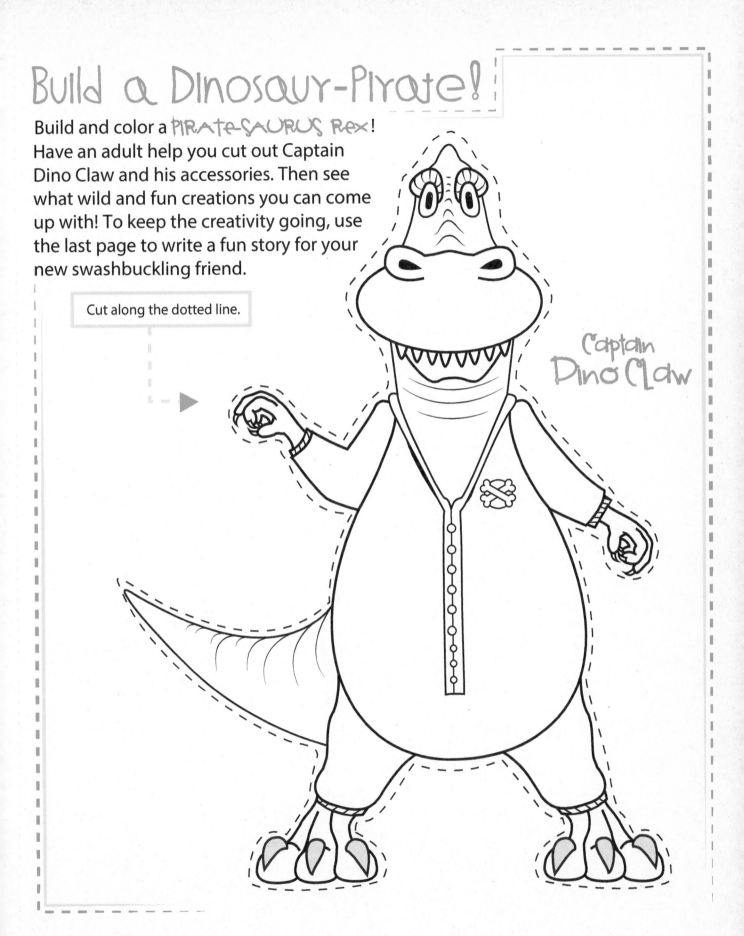

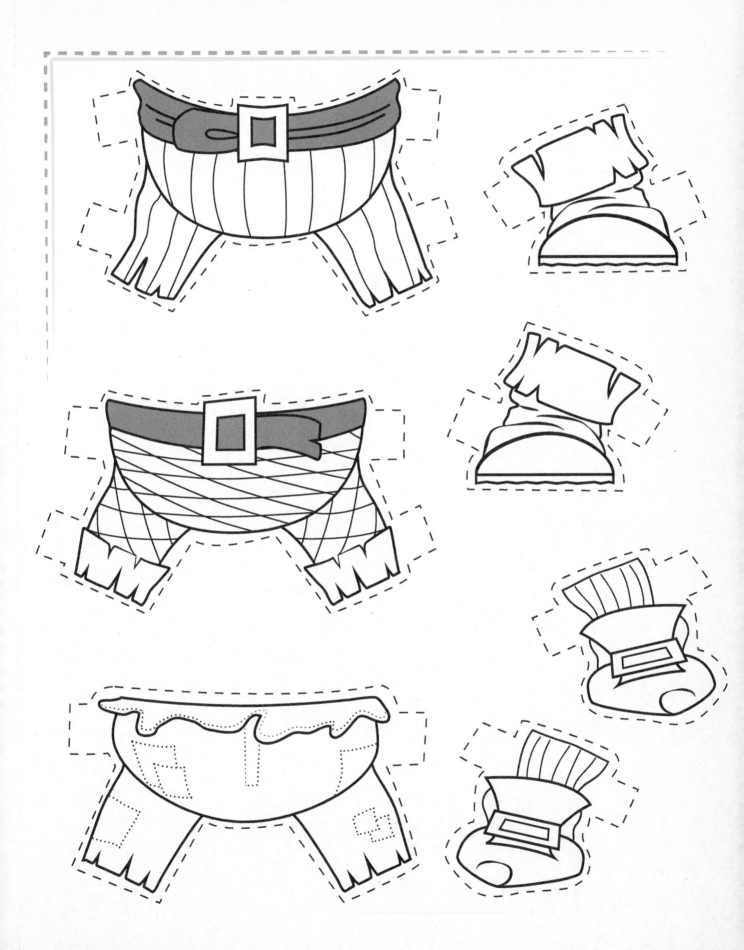

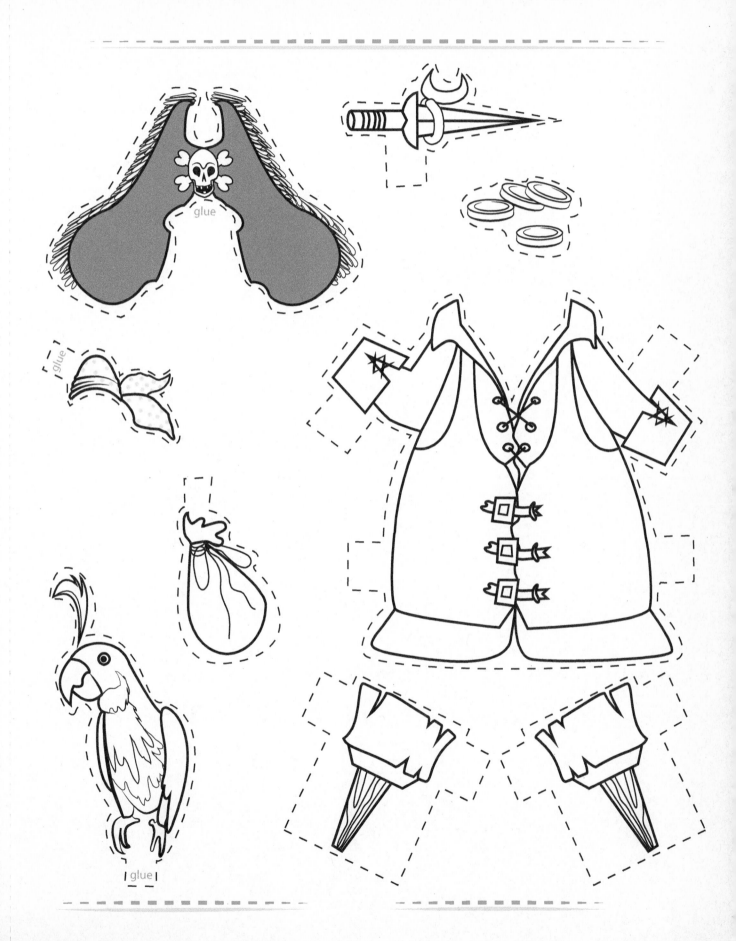

glue

glue

glue

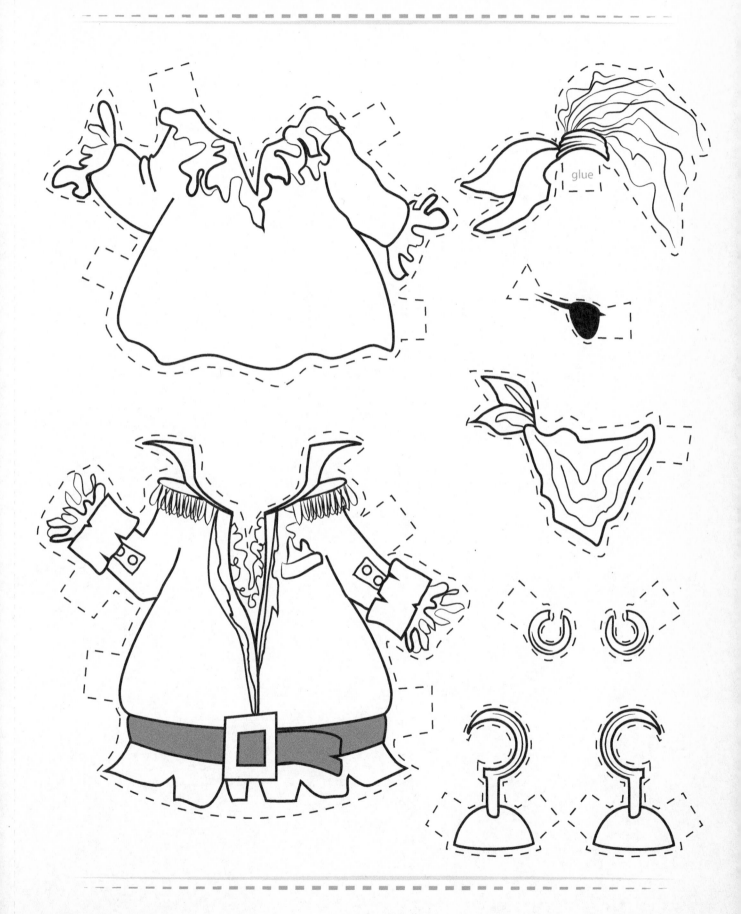

glue

119

WRITING PROMPT

Once your pirate is done, think of a fun adventure that he could go on, and write a story about it!